Starting Out On Your Own
A guide to smart living when starting out on your own

Kim L Davis

Disclaimer: The author disclaim as far as is legally permissible, all liability for accidents or injuries or loss that may occur as a result of information or instructions given in this book. Stay within the law and local rules, and be considerate of other people.

No part of this publication may be reproduced, stored in a retrieval system or transmitted in any form or by any means, electronic, mechanical, photocopying, recording, or otherwise, without the written permission of the publisher.

Copyright © 2013 Kim L. Davis

All rights reserved.

ISBN-10: 0615790194
ISBN-13: 9780615790190

DEDICATION

I dedicate this guide to my wonderful children Arondo, Candace, Harold III and my husband Harold Davis Jr. The journey through life with you is wonderful. Thank you for your love.

****

Thank you God.

CONTENTS

	Acknowledgments	i
Chapter 1	Introduction	1
Chapter 2	Ready Set Go	2
Chapter 3	Faith	3
Chapter 4	Choices	4
Chapter 5	Maturity	6
Chapter 6	Family Matters	8
Chapter 7	Housing	10
Chapter 8	Friends	12
Chapter 9	Truth	14
Chapter 10	Money	15
Chapter 11	Sex	18
Chapter 12	Children	20
Chapter 13	Education	22
Chapter 14	Employment	24
Chapter 15	Drugs and Alcohol	26
Chapter 16	The Law	28
Chapter 17	Love	29

Chapter 18	Marriage	31
Chapter 19	Transportation	33
Chapter 20	Vacation	34
Chapter 21	Health	35
Chapter 22	Enjoy Life	38

ACKNOWLEDGMENTS

This book would not have been possible without the support of my husband, Harold. Thank you for understanding my long nights at the computer. God makes all things possible.

1

INTRODUCTION

Life is something like school. It is full of valuable lessons to learn. Some classes have to be repeated in order to pass and go to the next level. I was inspired to write this book while looking back over my life at the things that I learned and the things I wished I had learned. I looked back and wondered if I had known certain things, would I have made different or better decisions? I would say yes. I hope this guide will help you make good decisions in your journey of life. The chapters are not in any particular order, read them as needed.

****

My desire for all young adults is that you would take time to invest in yourself. Enjoy life and do not settle into a marriage like relationship or marriage before you know yourself and have experienced your own desires. Marriage is a wonderful experience, but you should be ready for it.

2

READY SET GO

If you are reading this book you have started thinking about the next step in your journey of life or someone wants you to start thinking about it. However you reached this point, welcome to an exciting life adventure. One thing that you should know is that your life will not be like anyone else's. It is yours to shape and mold. Life is full of desirable and undesirable outcomes. It is all about how you approach them. Take control, be responsible and remember the things you already know.

****

If You Are Going To Leave, Leave Well Equipped.

3

FAITH

Some will disagree with me on this, but I believe that if you ground yourself in knowing God and have faith in God's existence, you will find comfort and peace as you journey through life. The relationship you have with Christ will strengthen your ability to get through difficult times.

****

If you would like a Bible, visit a local church.

4

CHOICES

Everything we do involves making a choice. Sometimes you make the choice and at other times someone else makes the choice for you. You should make more of your own choices as you mature. Remember that every choice you make has a consequence. The consequence can be good or bad and affect you for life. So don't make choices that give you short-term gratification and long term heartaches.

For example, you are in school and your friends keep having plans during one of your class hours. You make a choice to skip class sometimes to go with your friends. Next thing you know you have failed the class. You now have to take the class over, your grade point average suffers, you have to stay longer in school, you or someone else has to pay for the class and you disappoint yourself and others. Guess what you should do now? LEARN from your mistakes and MOVE ON. Go to your classes and do the best you can. Stay focused on completing your education. Don't get stuck in a pity party. The longer you dwell on the circumstances, the longer you stay in them. Remember the choices you make today will manifest later in your life.

****

Make the choice to overcome life's obstacles and remember if you are alive to make the choice, you have been given a chance to overcome whatever you are faced with.

****

Have your voice heard. Register to vote and get out and vote.

****

Make the choice to be happy. Make the choice to do good. Make the choice to love and be loved.

5

MATURITY

Sometimes turning 18 gives you a sense of feeling that you are grown up and mature. When this happens things are said and done that were not said and done before. People's feelings get hurt. Unless something remarkable happened over night, you are the same person you were 24 hours earlier. If you had to hide your actions or refrain from doing certain things before you turned 18, what makes it all right to do them after you turned 18? Respecting others never changes no matter how old you are.

****

If you are getting help with food, car payments, school tuition, clothes, phone bill, car insurance, medical bills, etc., YOU ARE NOT INDEPENDENT. Getting help from someone does not mean you are not mature, but the way you handle your life and make decisions is a reflection on how well you are maturing.

****

You should not turn down constructive advice. The person giving you advice should not try to run your life, but if you had all the answers you would not need their help. You can tell the difference between someone trying to run your life and someone caring about you. Bottom line is that sometimes you have to listen and do things that you may not want to do. That is a sign of maturity.

****

The path to maturity begins with being responsible for yourself and your actions, taking care of yourself physically and financially and being able to survive in our society in a positive manner.

****

Volunteer and help others.

****

Say "Thank You." So many times we forget to say those simple words that mean so much.

6

FAMILY MATTERS

Whether you like it or not your family is what you get. You may not get along at all times, but do not let life's issues separate you from your family. Don't stop speaking to a family member because he or she would not co-sign a loan for you. Don't stop visiting your parents because they do not like your significant other. Your desires are just that, yours. Do not expect other people to have the same likes or dislikes. As long as you are being respected you have to learn to live with differences and disagreements.

****

Respect your parents at all times. Your parents may not do what you like them to do or what you thought they should have done, but they raised you. Regroup and apologize. It will make you feel so much better.

****

What can make you stop speaking to your brother or sister forever? Let's face it--things happen, people make mistakes, you make mistakes. Forgiveness is one of the hardest things to do, but when you learn to forgive those that hurt you, you will have defeated one of the stress factors in your life. What I have found out is that when you hold on to hurt and pain it consumes your life. Look at this scenario for an example:

> A family member is having a party and a person that you don't speak to anymore is going to be there. You spend time debating whether you are even going to attend the party. You are consumed with thoughts of "what if" scenarios. You get to the event and don't enjoy yourself because of your thoughts about that person. After the party you are upset about what did or did not happen with this person.

Look at how much time and energy you spent on not speaking to someone. Mend the relationship and enjoy the next party.

****

Stay in touch with your family. Pick up the phone and call to say "Hello."

****

The burdens of the heart can consume your mind. You don't want the day to come where you have to say, " I wish I had told....". Tell them today.

7

HOUSING

You may dream and desire to grow up and have your own home. In reality, it takes time to be on your own. Your only option may be to stay with your parents or someone else longer than you had planned.

****

When you live with others and have a job and money to spend on going out, buying gadgets, clothes, etc, then you should be able to help out with the expenses of their home. It is not the amount that you have to offer; it is showing maturity and responsibility that is important.

****

Treat people's property with respect. If you did not buy it, you have no right to misuse it. Let me put it another way, even if you bought it and you are living in someone else's house, you have to refrain from destroying your stuff on their property.

****

No you cannot shack up in my house! Your significant other cannot sleep over. As a matter of fact, don't lie around, sit around and act disrespectful. Many times when we reach a certain age we think that we should be able to do what we want. In some cases that is correct, but if you do not have your own place, do not disrespect someone else's home. No one wants to see you lounging around doing things that should be done in private.

****

When you are looking for an apartment or house, you should know what you can comfortably afford. This means that you can pay the rent with the income you make from one job, not overtime or a second job. You must have a job first before you attempt to move into your own place. Remember to include in your calculation your car payment, insurance, phone bill, gas, electric, food and hobby. If this is done before you enter into a rental agreement you will avoid the stress of not knowing how you are going to pay your bills. You should also avoid having a roommate that does not have a stable job to fulfill his or her part of the rental agreement. If you do have a roommate put the terms of paying the bills in writing.

****

Keep your house clean. Clutter and filthiness can affect your mood and attract unwanted pests.

8

FRIENDS

Having a friend is a two-way relationship. You should not call someone your friend when he or she does not have the same mutual feelings. Friendship is built on trust.

****

Keep friends out of your romantic relationship. Actually a true friend will not intrude on your relationship. He or she will be there for support, to listen and give his or her honest opinion without trying to destroy your relationship.

****

A significant other can come between friends. Do not get involved with anyone that your friend ever dated, even if it was years ago. Remember nothing stays a secret.

****

A friend will be there for you no matter what the situation

is. Don't measure your friendship by what someone does for you. Friendship is such a special relationship and can last through good and bad times. If you are fortunate to develop a friendship, cherish it.

****

A friend does not care about how many times he or she had to help you; a friend cares about how he or she can help you.

****

9

TRUTH

One of the most important things that you have control over in your life is your character. Tell the truth. Don't lie. A lie never dies. Do not lean on the excuse that you told a lie so you would not hurt someone. The lie you tell will hurt you in the long run. Have you ever heard the saying that "a lie will grow"? You will have to tell another lie to cover up the first lie and the pattern keeps going.

****

If someone asks you to lie or cover up something, you should question his or her character and evaluate your relationship.

10

MONEY

It is a good idea to take a class on finance and money. It will be the best investment that you make for yourself and it will pay for itself immediately. Having money and using it wisely is a fundamental necessity. Our economy runs on money and you need it to survive.

****

The abuse of money can lead you down a path of disaster. You should not love money to the point that you let money guide your actions in life.

****

Learning how to manage your money will allow you to reap the benefits of having good credit. You should try to establish good credit. You need one major credit card. Do not get pulled into applying for store credit cards. The interest is too high. Take the financial class. It will help you make good money decisions. Bad credit can delay the dream of being independent.

****

One very important thing to remember is "Don't Spend What You Don't Have". If you have to borrow money to purchase something that is not a necessity, you probably cannot afford to have it at that time and need to wait.

****

Sign up for free reward cards and restaurant clubs for the businesses that you frequently support. You can save money and earn free items.

****

If your funds are tight, do not eat out. Buy food and cook. Take your lunch to work. When you eat out ask for a glass of water instead of a beverage and eat dessert at home. You will be surprised at how much money you save.

****

If you borrow money from someone, regardless of who it is, pay him or her back. If you cannot pay the person all at once, pay the debt back a little at a time. Let the person know that you have not forgotten that you owe him or her money and that you intend to repay what you owe.

****

Obtain a copy of your credit report every year. The Fair Credit Reporting Act requires the major reporting companies to provide you with a free copy of your credit report once every 12 months.

Kim L. Davis

****

Open a bank account and save money. The sooner you start saving the better off you will be later. It is never too soon or too late to start saving money.

11

SEX

Sex is supposed to be an enjoyable experience. The best way to enjoy sex is to wait until you are married. When you wait the experience will be your first and the best because you will not have any other experience to compare it to. Your body will be pure for your spouse.

****

Unprotected sex can lead to death. HIV and other sexually transmitted diseases do not discriminate. You cannot tell if someone has a disease, the person may not know it either. Birth control does not protect you from getting a disease. If you are going to have sex with different partners, PROTECT YOURSELF.

****

Unplanned pregnancies can change your life drastically.

The reality is that if you have unprotected sex, the pregnancy is not unplanned because you make the choice to have unprotected sex. If you are struggling with taking care of yourself, you cannot take care of anyone else. The responsibility of taking care of a child should be shared by the mother and father. It is not a compromise, it is a fact. Your parents are not responsible for taking care of your child. They do not have to volunteer to babysit or do other things that you think they should do. This happens naturally with grandparents and family members, but it is not their responsibility.

****

Sex is such a delicate topic. It has a different meaning and experience for each individual person. Having sex with someone does not mean he or she loves you. It is very important to protect your body and heart from being misused.

12

CHILDREN

If you have a child your focus should be on providing him or her with the best care possible. Your desires do not have to be forgotten, but they have to be put into perspective. What this means is that you have to choose what is right for your child over what you want to do. If what you want to do and what is right for your child cannot be done together, then you should choose to do what is in the best interest of your child. Remember your child did not choose to come into this world. He or she was chosen to come into this world with you as his or her parent. Provide your child with a healthy environment. Do not expose him or her to drugs, cursing or any inappropriate behavior.

****

Children need to be raised. They need guidance and direction. They need you to have an expectation of them. Give them rules and boundaries. Tell them what you expect from them.

****

No your child is not always right. Let go of the "it's my child and I will correct them" attitude. We tend to get an attitude when someone tries to correct our child. If your child is wrong, get over it and let him or her be corrected. I am not talking about physical correction, which is another issue for you to handle.

****

Your home should be where your child learns good values, manners, how to love and how to be respectful. There is an old saying, "the apple does not fall far from the apple tree." If you never heard this it means the child is the apple and you are the apple tree and they get their behavior from you. Invest in your child, pay attention to him or her.

****

Give your child chores. Having responsibilities builds character and helps them become responsible.

****

It is OK to give your child things he or she desires, BUT if your child is disrespectful, disobedient and doing poorly in school, you should not reward bad behavior. Do not get caught up in giving your child things because you did not have them. This can cause you to overlook their behavior.

13

EDUCATION

You must obtain a High School diploma. The world is saturated with educated people. You will be overlooked for jobs because you do not have the basics. You may be one of the fortunate ones who get the chance to work your way up in a company, but you have to get in first. You may be able to get a job that does not require a specific skill and pays minimum wage. Is that your dream for your life? There is a need for people for unskilled jobs, but don't start life out settling for the least when you can strive for the best.

****

Whether you plan on acquiring a skill from going to college or taking up a trade, it is very important to have an education. Obtaining additional education is always a good thing, but try not to go in debt while getting an education. Community colleges offer classes at a much cheaper rate. If you work at a company that offers educational benefits, take advantage of them. If your parents have saved for you to go to school, do it and don't mess up.

****

Apply for financial aid using the Free Application for Federal Student Aid, (FAFSA). You can qualify for grants that you do not have to pay back and loans that you have to repay. You do not have to accept financial aid just because you qualify for it, but it is better to see what you qualify for than to not look at all.

****

Learn a second language. It is an asset in the job market and in our inter-connected world.

****

If you have a college degree and a clean record, try substitute teaching.

****

Learn to listen.

14

EMPLOYMENT

Have you heard someone say, "I am not working here because they don't pay enough" and they don't have a job? What is the logic behind this statement? If you don't have a job you need to take what you can get and continue to look for something better. Unless you are born into money or willingly supported by another person and do not have to work, you need to get a job. Really, even if someone is going to work everyday for you to enjoy a roof over your head and you do not have any obligations that keep you from working, get a job.

****

Prepare for interviews. Look over your resume. Do not put information on the resume that is not true. Dress neatly. Research the company that you are interviewing with. Make sure you answer the interview questions. It is acceptable to ask for clarity if you do not understand the question. Call or send a follow up letter. Ask if they have made a hiring decision. This is not being pushy--this is being assertive and proactive about your future.

****

A government job is an excellent choice. Try and get one right out of high school. You can move around and the benefits are good. High school students can get summer jobs with the government. Many times when they graduate, they are converted to full-time employees.

****

The best time to look for new opportunities is when you have a job. Do not quit your job if you do not have another opportunity secured.

****

When you have a job, do your job well. You are getting paid for it. Most companies exist to make a profit and not cater to you. Make changes where you can, accept the things you cannot change, or move on. This does not mean accept bad treatment or be disrespected. Work by example.

****

Do not burn your bridges. Always leave an open door or window in case you need to go back to a previous employer.

****

Do not step on people to get to the top.

15

DRUGS AND ALCOHOL

We grow up in a society that allows drugs and alcohol to flow freely through our neighborhoods. You do not have to take part in the use of socially accepted drugs and alcohol. You do not have to go along with the crowd. It is unfortunate that some people get addicted to drugs and alcohol. But some do not. Do you really want to take the chance to see which one you will be--addicted or non-addicted?

****

If you choose to drink, pay attention to your drinking habits. If you find yourself drinking everyday, you may have a problem. If you find yourself drinking whenever alcohol is around, evaluate the situation. You may have a problem. Do not be afraid to seek help. If you cannot control yourself when you drink, stop drinking. There was an old saying "whatever you do when you get drunk is the real you." Becoming addicted to drugs or alcohol can cause a financial disaster. It can destroy you, your family and friends.

****

DO NOT DRINK AND DRIVE.

*****

Just because you turn 21 does not mean you have to drink. Remember age 21 also means adult consequences if things go wrong.

*****

Smoking is bad for your health and can be bad for others around you. If you smoke, make an effort to quit. The smell of cigarette smoke stays on your clothes and lingers in your home. You may not smell it, but others do.

16

THE LAW

Laws are made to protect the population as a whole. Stealing, killing, doing drugs, speeding, and other acts are illegal. Illegal means against the law. Do not try to justify any illegal act that you have the ability to not do in the first place. You must obey the law. Our criminal system is not always fair and mistakes do happen. If you obey the law you have a better chance of not subjecting yourself to being involved in the system. Stay away from others who are doing illegal actions. Being in the wrong place or with the wrong crowd can cause you hardship. If your friends are drinking and driving, do not go with them. If you really care about your friends try to stop them from driving. Remember you have a choice. It is a tough call with peer pressure, but it is better to be a living friend than a dead friend.

****

Obtain valid identification and carry it with you at all times.

17

LOVE

Love is complicated to explain. Love is the act of doing, caring and sharing. You have to nurture it. Love does not come with conditions. Love does not require you to hurt yourself. Love produces feeling, but love is not a feeling. Feelings change and we tend to react to feelings. We usually only hear people talk about love when they are talking about a relationship. That is because people relate the feelings of happiness, joy, butterflies, and desire to love. You must understand that love is more than that. I encourage you to seek the true meaning - for God is love.

****

You must love yourself before you can love anyone else. I do not mean being selfish or wanting good only for yourself. Loving yourself means taking care of your body, soul and heart. Surround yourself with good and positive things and you will be able to share these things with others.

****

Your love for your parents, mate, siblings, family, friends and children are of different qualities and should not be compared. Mistakes can happen in relationships when someone tries to test the love of a significant other and their parents. It is the wrong approach to whatever issues you are having and could ruin your relationship.

****

You cannot earn love. Do not think that the more things you do for someone the more it will make that person love you. Actions are done because of love, but not to earn love.

****

Love is contagious; if you catch it you can spread it.

18

MARRIAGE

Marry who you want, want who you marry. Marriage is a covenant and not a contract. It is as important to be the right person for someone else, as it is to find the right person. There will always be more things to want in life. As you mature in your life you will understand the importance of being content with what you have and working to make the best of your situation.

****

Being married is not all about you. It is about you and your spouse satisfying each other. It is about going through life together and serving each other. Just think about it. If you are trying to please each other then both people's needs are being fulfilled. Selfishness is one of the main issues to come between couples. Communication, trust and forgiveness are important to keeping a marriage healthy.

****

You should not marry for the wrong reasons. Before you marry make sure you are committed to making the marriage work. It does not matter what your friends or family want. A marriage will be between you and your spouse. Remember the person you are going to marry is going to be the same person after you marry him or her. Do not expect the person to change because you married him or her. It is true when you hear people say "you knew what you were getting before you got married." If you are having mixed feeling, then postpone the wedding and work out the issues before you make that big commitment. Marriage is beautiful and can bring you a lifetime of fulfillment and companionship.

****

Get your finances together before you get married. Money is one of the most common causes of marital issues.

****

Before you get married have a discussion with your significant other about children. Don't assume that he or she wants to have children because you are getting married.

19

TRANSPORTATION

It is nice to have the type of vehicle that you want, but sometimes that desire has to wait. You should not enter into a car payment agreement that cost more than your rent. It is better to buy a used vehicle and save your money to get your dream car. Your car payment could cause you to have to work overtime and miss out on enjoying the car you purchased. Pay attention to the interest rate of your agreement. Car dealers will give you that eye-catching car, but you will be paying dearly with the interest they will charge you. Better yet, use public transportation and save for a car.

****

If you have a car, make sure you have car insurance. Drive safely and obey the laws. Do not text or do other distracting activities while driving. Getting traffic citations and having accidents can cause you to have high insurance premiums. If you are on someone else's insurance plan and have accidents, the policy holder's insurance can go up.

20

VACATION

Relaxation is a major factor in having a balanced life. You should take time out for yourself, even if you do not go anywhere. You need the mental break time. If you have a family, vacation time is a time for bonding and sharing special experiences.

****

Whatever you do, do not let paid vacation time go unused. If you are working that much, stop and take a look at your life.

21

HEALTH

Your health is so important that you should make sure you get a physical examination every year. You do not want to have a disease and find out about it when it is in a stage where your options to control or cure it are limited.

****

If you do not have health insurance, there are free health clinics.

****

Did you know that a lot of diseases can be managed with a change in life style?

****

Your weight can increase your chances of developing certain diseases. Some diseases are hereditary, but being over weight can be a contributing factor. Sometimes weight gain can be due to medical issues and that is why you should stay on top of your health. We get very touchy when someone talks about being over weight. The truth is we get offended. Get over it, face it and start making small changes. You will see the difference it makes and you will feel good about it.

****

Yes, you should love who you are and that should include loving your body. Everyone is not going to be thin, but we can all strive to be healthier.

****

Some health plans will pay for weight loss programs if your doctor states that your weight puts you at high risk for certain diseases. Don't be embarrassed to take care of yourself.

****

Exercise as much as you can. Walking is a great means of getting exercise. Exercising builds up your heart and helps your body perform its normal functions.

****

Eat healthy. Eating fruits and vegetables will give you the nutrients that your body needs to function. Eat breakfast. You should not skip meals. Did you know that when you starve your body, it stores fat? Lay off the fatty foods and sweets. Bad foods not only hinder your cells from functioning to their highest potential, they manifest themselves by adding pounds to our body. It is never to late to start eating healthier. You can start slow by cutting back one item at a time. If you just stop drinking soda and drinks high in sugar you will notice a difference in your weight. Eating healthier does not mean you have to give up all of your favorite foods. It means learning to eat all foods in moderation.

Kim L. Davis

****

Take care of your teeth and gums. Poor oral hygiene can lead to other diseases.

22

ENJOY LIFE

Life is full of ups and downs. Everything will not go your way. You have a choice to take control of your life. When things happen that cause you a set back, don't stay back. Pick yourself up and move forward. Learn from the mistakes that you make and don't repeat them. Don't judge. Keep hate out of your life. Share with others. Help others. You will be surprised at how helping others will help you to focus less on your issues. It will make you appreciate your life. Don't make everything so complicated by reading into things too much. Trust in your instinct and believe in yourself.

Love is so powerful, love and be loved. Enjoy life.

****

Seek God and He will direct your path.

NOTES

HOW WILL YOU START OUT ON YOUR OWN?

www.ingramcontent.com/pod-product-compliance
Lightning Source LLC
Chambersburg PA
CBHW061302040426
42444CB00010B/2484